AF408509

Trading For Newbies

Jackson Brooks

Jackson Brooks

First edition
All Rights Reserved
Author: © Jackson Brooks

Reproduction of this book in whole or in part, or its transmission by any means, is prohibited without the express written permission of the author. Any unauthorized use constitutes an infringement of copyright.

Copyright holder: © Julian Velandia

Index

Financial Markets Explained

Financial markets are places where people buy and sell things called financial assets, such as stocks, currencies, bonds, and cryptocurrencies. A financial asset is something that has value and that people are willing to buy or sell, hoping to make money from its change in price. Imagine a big fruit market, but instead of fruit, you trade these things that, even though you can't hold them in your hands, represent money. These markets are huge, and the best thing is that anyone with internet access can participate from home.

In financial markets, every asset has a price that goes up and down, depending on how many people want to buy or sell it at any given time. If a lot of people are interested in buying, the price goes up. If a lot of people want to sell, the price goes down. This happens because prices in financial markets work the same as in any other market: if something is in high demand, it becomes more expensive, and if no one wants it, it goes down in price. The trick to trading is to try to buy when prices are low and sell when they are high.

There are several types of financial markets, and each one specializes in different types of assets. The stock market, for example, is where people buy and sell parts of companies. When you buy a share, you're buying a small part of that company. If the company is doing well, the value of its shares goes up, and you make money. But if the company isn't doing so well, the value of its shares goes down, and you can lose money.

Another important market is the foreign exchange market, also known as Forex. Here, instead of companies, individuals buy and sell currencies from different countries, such as dollars, euros or yen. People make money in this market by taking advantage of changes in the value of currencies. For example, if the dollar rises against the euro, a trader who bought dollars and sold euros can make money. It's like exchanging money when you travel, but here you do it to try to make a profit.

We also have the bond market, which is a little more complicated to understand, but very important. A bond is basically a loan that you give to a government or a company, and they promise to pay you back with a little interest. People buy and sell bonds in the financial market, trying to make money from changes in interest. This market is more popular with investors looking for something safer, because bonds are usually less risky than stocks or currencies.

Finally, there is the cryptocurrency market, which has gained a lot of popularity in recent years. In this market, digital currencies such as Bitcoin, Ethereum, and many others are bought and sold. Unlike traditional currencies, cryptocurrencies are not controlled by governments or banks, which makes them a very different and sometimes very risky asset. Their prices can change very quickly, which attracts some traders who are looking to take advantage of those quick movements to make money.

The most interesting thing about financial markets is that they are all connected in some way. A major event in the world, such as an economic crisis or news about a famous company, can affect all markets at the same time. That's why it's important for traders to pay attention to the news and understand how different events can influence the market they're trading on.

In short, financial markets are places where people buy and sell assets in the hope of making money when their prices change. There are many types of markets, each specializing in different types of assets, such as stocks, currencies, bonds, or cryptocurrencies. Although it may seem complicated at first, understanding how markets work is the first step to becoming a successful trader. It just takes patience, observation, and, above all, practice to start navigating this exciting world.

Basic Tools for the Trader

When you decide to start trading, it's like embarking on a new adventure, and for that adventure you need the right tools. Just like a carpenter needs his hammer and saw, a trader needs certain resources to operate in the financial markets. These basic tools are not complicated, but they are essential for you to be able to do your job well. Here I will explain what they are and how you can start using them.

The main tool you are going to use as a trader is a trading platform. Think of this platform as the place where you are going to do all your trading. It is like your office or your control center. On this platform, you will be able to view price charts, analyze asset movement, make your purchases and sales, and review your results. There are many different platforms, but most of them work in a similar way. Some of the most well-known ones are MetaTrader, TradingView, or Thinkorswim. These platforms can seem a little intimidating at first, but once you get the hang of them, you will realize that they are quite easy to use.

Within the trading platform, one of the first things you will learn to use is price charts. These charts are visualizations of the price behavior of an asset over time. They can be lines, bars, or candles, and they show you how the price of an asset has changed over minutes, hours, days, or even months. Charts are like a map that will guide you in making decisions. If you learn to read them correctly, you will be able to identify when it is a good time to buy or sell.

Another basic tool you will find on your platform is technical indicators. These are tools that help you analyze price charts. For example, some indicators will tell you if the price of an asset is rising too fast or if it is about to fall. There are many types of indicators, but the most common and easy to use are moving averages, RSI (relative strength index), and MACD (moving average convergence/divergence). Don't worry if you don't understand how they work at first. As you practice, you will become familiar with them and know when they are giving you important signals.

In addition to charts and indicators, another tool that will be useful to you is the economic calendar. This calendar tells you when important news is going to be released that can affect the markets. For example, if the government is going to announce data on employment or inflation, the prices of certain assets are likely to change. Being aware of this news will help you avoid unpleasant surprises and make more informed decisions. Many traders check the economic calendar every day before they start trading, to make sure there are no unexpected events that can affect their trades.

One aspect that we cannot ignore is risk management, and for this, the key tool that you are going to use is the stop loss. A stop loss is an order that you give to the platform to automatically close a trade if the price goes against you. For example, if you buy a stock and the price starts to drop too much, the stop loss will sell that stock before you lose too much money. It is like a safety belt for your trades. Many beginner traders make the mistake of not using a stop loss and, as a result, their losses accumulate. Therefore, it is important that you learn how to use this tool from the beginning.

In addition to these tools, it is also helpful to have a trading notebook or journal. Although this is not a digital tool, it is essential so that you can keep track of all your trades. Writing down what you did well and what you did wrong will help you improve over time. Some traders also use spreadsheets to keep a detailed record of their profits and losses. The important thing is that you have a system where you can review your progress and learn from your mistakes.

Last but not least, we cannot forget about demo accounts. A demo account is a trading account that allows you to trade with fictitious money. It is the best tool to practice without risking your real money. With a demo account, you can familiarize yourself with the platform, try out different strategies, and learn how the markets work without the pressure of losing money. Many platforms offer this option, and it is a great way to gain confidence before trading in the real market.

In summary, the basic tools for a trader include the trading platform, price charts, technical indicators, economic calendar, stop loss, a trading journal, and if you are just starting out, a demo account. All of these tools will help you make smarter decisions and protect your money while you learn how to trade. It may seem like a lot of information at first, but with time and practice, all of these tools will become part of your daily routine as a trader. So don't be afraid to explore them and start using them.

Which is Best for You?

When you enter the world of trading, one of the first questions you'll probably ask yourself is: what type of trading is best for me? The answer to this question will depend on a number of factors, including your personality, the time you have available, your risk tolerance, and your financial goals. There are different trading styles, and each has its advantages and disadvantages. Let's explore some of the most common ones so you can find out which one best suits you.

One of the most popular types of trading is day trading, which involves buying and selling assets on the same day. Day traders don't leave their trades open overnight; everything is closed before the market day ends. This type of trading is ideal for people who like to be in front of a computer for several hours a day and make quick decisions. If you're someone who enjoys action and constant movement, day trading might be for you. However, this style also requires a great deal of focus and ability to manage stress, as markets can move quickly and decisions need to be made in a matter of minutes or even seconds. If you like a challenge and have the time to dedicate several hours a day, you might consider trying day trading.

Another style of trading is swing trading, which is a bit more relaxed than day trading. In swing trading, trades are held open for several days or even weeks. Swing traders try to take advantage of medium-term price movements. Unlike day trading, swing traders are not glued to the screen all day. This style is ideal for people who don't have as much time, but still want to actively participate in the markets. If you have a full-time job or can't dedicate several hours a day to trading, swing trading might be an attractive option for you. The pace is slower and you have more time to analyze your trades before making decisions.

There is also scalping, which is one of the fastest forms of trading. Scalping involves making many trades in a very short period of time, often holding a position for only a few minutes or even seconds. Scalpers look for small profits on each trade, but make up for it by making many trades per day. This style is perfect for people who enjoy a fast pace and have the ability to make instant decisions. However, it also requires a great deal of focus and discipline, as profits per trade are usually small. Scalping is not for everyone, but if you like the adrenaline rush and prefer to get in and out of the market quickly, it could be an interesting option for you.

Another style of trading is position trading, which is the opposite of scalping in many ways. Position traders hold their trades open for weeks, months, or even years. These traders are not interested in the daily movements of the market; instead, they focus on long-term trends. This type of trading is ideal for people who have a lot of patience and do not want to constantly monitor the markets. If you prefer to make long-term decisions and do not mind waiting to see the results, position trading might be your style. Additionally, this type of trading is usually less stressful since you do not need to keep an eye on the daily fluctuations of the market all the time.

An important point to consider is your **risk tolerance**. Some trading styles, such as scalping and day trading, can be riskier because the market moves are fast and abrupt. If you are uncomfortable with the idea of losing money in a short period of time, these styles may not be for you. On the other hand, if you prefer a more conservative approach with less risk, swing trading or position trading may be more suitable.

It's also important to think about the **time** you can devote to trading. If you have a full-time job or a lot of other responsibilities, you probably don't have time to do day trading or scalping, which require you to be available during the day. In this case, swing trading or position trading, which are more flexible in terms of time, might fit better with your lifestyle.

In addition to time and risk tolerance, also consider your **personality**. Some people enjoy the thrill of quick decisions, while others prefer to carefully analyze each move before acting. The type of trading you choose should match your personality so that you enjoy the process. If you are someone who is comfortable with chaos and speed, then scalping or day trading may be exciting for you. If you prefer to take your time, swing trading or position trading could make you feel calmer and more in control.

In the end, there is no right or wrong answer. The best type of trading for you is the one that fits your needs, personality, and lifestyle. Some traders try out several styles before deciding what works best for them. Most importantly, remember that no matter what type of trading you choose, the key is to keep learning, practicing, and continually improving. Trading is not a sprint, but rather a marathon where you discover what works best for you as you go.

Reading Price Charts

Learning how to read price charts is like learning to read a new language in the world of trading. It can seem confusing at first, but once you understand it, it is one of the most powerful tools you have at your disposal. Price charts show you how an asset behaves over time and help you make decisions about when to buy or sell. In this chapter, we are going to explain how these charts work in a simple and straightforward way, so that you can start reading them without any problems.

First, it's important to understand what a price chart is. A price chart is simply a visual representation of the price of an asset, such as a stock or cryptocurrency, over time. The vertical axis of the chart shows the price, while the horizontal axis shows time. So, by looking at a chart, you can see how the price of that asset has changed over minutes, hours, days, or even months, depending on the time scale you choose. This representation allows you to identify patterns and trends, which is key to making smart trading decisions.

The most common and useful type of chart you'll encounter is a **candlestick chart**, also known as a Japanese candlestick chart. This chart is made up of a series of "candlesticks," which are small rectangles with thin lines above and below them, and each of these candlesticks represents a certain period of time, which could be a minute, an hour, a day, etc. The candlestick tells you a lot about what happened to the price during that time. For example, if the candlestick is green (or white on some charts), it means that the price rose during that period. If the candlestick is red (or black), it means that the price fell.

Each candle has four key points that you need to understand: the open, the close, the high, and the low. The open price is the price at which the candle started in that time period, and the close price is where it ended. If the candle is green, the close price will be above the open price, meaning the price rose. If it is red, the close price will be below the open, indicating the price fell. The thin lines coming out of the top and bottom of the candle are called shadows, and they show you the highest and lowest price the asset reached during that time period. So, a candle with long shadows indicates that the price varied a lot, while a candle with short shadows means the price remained fairly stable.

Candlestick charts are very popular because, with just a quick glance, they allow you to see not only whether the price went up or down, but also how much it changed and how volatile the market was during that period. If you see a lot of green candles in a row, that could indicate an uptrend, meaning prices are steadily rising. Conversely, if you see a series of red candles, you're probably seeing a downtrend, suggesting prices are falling. Spotting these trends will help you know if it's a good time to buy or sell.

Another important thing you'll notice when reading charts is that prices don't move in a straight line. Markets are constantly moving, and prices rise and fall irregularly. That's why when you look at a chart, you'll notice peaks and valleys forming. These peaks are called resistances, and valleys are called supports. Resistance is a price level where the asset seems to have a hard time continuing to rise. It's like a ceiling that the price can't easily break through. Support, on the other hand, is a level where the price stops falling and starts rising again, like a floor that prevents the price from falling further. Identifying these support and resistance levels is essential to knowing when to enter or exit a trade.

In addition to candlesticks and support and resistance levels, there are patterns that experienced traders look for on price charts. These patterns are figures that repeat over time and can give you clues about what might happen next. For example, one of the most well-known patterns is the **double top**, which occurs when the price rises twice to the same level, but fails to break that resistance and then falls. This pattern usually indicates that the price might continue to fall. Another common pattern is the **double bottom**, which is the opposite: the price falls twice to the same level, but does not fall any further and then starts to rise. This suggests that the price might start an uptrend.

There are also more advanced patterns, such as head and shoulders or triangles, that traders use to predict future price movements. But don't worry if all this seems a bit complicated at first. The important thing is to start getting familiar with the charts and practice reading them. Over time, you'll start noticing these patterns naturally, and you'll be able to use them to improve your trading decisions.

Once you're comfortable reading candlestick charts, you can also explore other chart types, such as bar charts or line charts. Bar charts are similar to candlesticks, but instead of using rectangles, they just have lines indicating the open, close, high, and low. Line charts, on the other hand, are much simpler and just show a line connecting closing prices over time. While these charts are easier to understand at a glance, they don't give you as much information as candlestick charts, which is why most traders prefer to use candlesticks.

In short, learning how to read price charts is a fundamental skill for any trader. Candlestick charts are the most common and useful tool for visualizing market movements. By learning how to read candlesticks, identify trends, and recognize patterns, you will be in a better position to make informed decisions about when to buy and sell. It may seem complicated at first, but with practice and patience, chart reading will become a natural and exciting part of your trading routine.

The Pillars of Technical Analysis

Technical analysis is one of the most widely used tools by traders to make market decisions. Instead of focusing on news or fundamental aspects of a company or asset, such as earnings or growth, technical analysis focuses on studying price charts and past market behavior. The idea is that prices move in patterns and that these patterns can repeat themselves, allowing you to predict what might happen in the future. In this chapter, we're going to explore the fundamental pillars of technical analysis, so you can understand how it works and how you can use it in your trading.

The first pillar of technical analysis is the idea that **price discounts everything**. This means that all relevant information about an asset, be it news, rumors, or expectations, is already reflected in the current price. According to this theory, you don't need to analyze external events to make trading decisions; everything you need is on the price chart. This makes technical analysis a very practical and accessible tool, as you don't have to worry about understanding every economic detail or news item that affects the market. You only need to focus on the price behavior.

The second pillar is that prices move in trends. This is crucial for any trader using technical analysis. Markets don't move randomly; they tend to follow clear directions over a period of time, either up (uptrend), down (downtrend), or sideways (no clear trend). If you can identify a trend, you can use it to your advantage by buying when the market is going up or selling when the market is going down. To identify these trends, traders use a variety of tools, such as moving averages, which smooth out price movements and help you see the general direction of the market. The key here is that once a trend forms, it's likely to continue in that direction until something causes it to change.

The third pillar of technical analysis is that **history tends to repeat itself**. This is based on the idea that humans, as a whole, tend to behave similarly in similar situations. In other words, emotions like fear and greed influence traders' behavior, and those emotions create chart patterns that repeat over time. If you can identify a pattern in the past that led to a certain price move, you might expect that when that pattern appears again, the market will behave in a similar way. This concept is the basis for many chart patterns that technical traders look for, such as the "double top" or "head-and-shoulders" pattern we mentioned earlier.

A fundamental aspect of technical analysis is **support and resistance levels**. Support is a price level where an asset tends to stop falling and bounce back up. It is like a floor that prevents the price from falling further. On the other hand, resistance is a level where the price has difficulty continuing to rise, as if there were a ceiling that the market cannot break. Traders look for these levels because they are important points where the price is likely to change direction. If the price is close to a support level, you might consider buying, hoping that the price will bounce back. If the price is close to a resistance level, you might sell, anticipating that the price will fall.

Another important pillar of technical analysis is **volume**. Volume is the amount of trades that are taking place in a certain asset over a period of time. When volume is high, it means there is a lot of interest in that asset, and when volume is low, it means there are not as many trades happening. Volume is important because it can confirm trends. For example, if the price is going up and the volume is also increasing, that could be a sign that the uptrend is strong and will continue. On the other hand, if the price is going up but the volume is decreasing, that could be a sign that the trend is losing steam and could reverse soon. Using volume as an additional tool in your technical analysis will give you a better idea of the strength of a trend.

Moving averages are another essential tool in technical analysis. A moving average is simply the average price of an asset over a certain number of days. For example, a 10-day moving average calculates the average of prices over the past 10 days. This helps you smooth out daily price fluctuations and see the overall trend. Moving averages are also used to identify entry and exit points in the market. When the price crosses above a moving average, it could be a buy signal, and when the price crosses below it, it could be a sell signal. Some traders use multiple moving averages at the same time to look for crossovers between them, which can be a sign that a trend change is coming.

One of the most commonly used tools by technical traders is technical indicators, which are mathematical calculations applied to price charts. These indicators help you identify potential trading opportunities. One of the most well-known is the Relative Strength Index (RSI), which measures whether an asset is overbought or oversold. If the RSI is very high, that could be a sign that the asset is overbought and the price could fall soon. If the RSI is very low, that could indicate that the asset is oversold and the price could rise. Another popular indicator is the MACD (Moving Average Convergence Divergence), which helps identify changes in the strength, direction, momentum, and duration of a trend.

Finally, technical analysis is not just about studying charts and applying tools. It also requires a good dose of **discipline and patience**. Traders who use technical analysis often face the temptation to make impulsive decisions based on sudden market movements. However, the most successful traders are those who follow their strategies carefully and stick to their rules, even when the market becomes volatile. It is important to remember that technical analysis is not an exact science and that no trading method guarantees profits. However, by applying these pillars and using tools such as trend analysis, support and resistance, volume, and chart patterns, you can increase your chances of making informed decisions and improve your trading success.

In summary, the pillars of technical analysis are based on three key ideas: that price discounts everything, that prices move in trends, and that history tends to repeat itself. By learning to identify trends, analyze support and resistance levels, and use tools like volume and technical indicators, you will be better equipped to navigate the financial markets and make better decisions.

Basic Chart Patterns

Basic chart patterns are one of the most important tools traders use to make decisions in the market. These patterns form on price charts due to the repetitive behavior of market participants, and traders study them to predict where the price of an asset might move. Understanding these patterns is like having a map that will guide you along the path of your trade, helping you identify potential buy or sell points. In this chapter, we are going to explore some of the most basic chart patterns and how you can use them in your trading strategy.

One of the most well-known chart patterns is the **double top**. This pattern is formed when the price of an asset rises to a certain level, then falls a little, and then rises back to the same level without being able to break it, forming two peaks that look like an "M". The double top indicates that the price is having difficulty breaking through a resistance level, which could mean that it is losing strength and is likely to go lower soon. It is as if the price tried to break through a barrier twice but failed both times, suggesting that buyers are losing momentum. Once the price falls after forming the second peak, it can be a signal to sell or exit a position, as the price is likely to continue falling.

At the other extreme, we have the **double bottom**, which is basically the opposite of the double top. This pattern is formed when the price drops to a low level, then rises a bit, and then drops back to the same level without being able to break that "floor", forming two valleys that look like a "W". The double bottom indicates that the price is finding a strong support level, suggesting that sellers are losing strength and the price might start to rise. This pattern is a bullish signal, and when the price rises after forming the second valley, it can be a good opportunity to buy, hoping that the price will continue its upward trend.

Another basic chart pattern is the **head-shoulders**, which is a bit more complicated but very popular among traders. This pattern forms when the price of an asset rises to a high level (the first shoulder), then drops a bit, then rises even higher (the head), and finally drops again before rising one last time to a lower level (the second shoulder). This pattern is a sign that the market might be changing from an uptrend to a downtrend. Traders interpret this pattern as an indication that the momentum of buyers is weakening, and when the price breaks the support level connecting the two shoulders, this can be a signal to sell, as the price is likely to continue falling.

The inverse pattern to the head and shoulders is the **inverted head and shoulders**, which, as the name implies, is simply the pattern in reverse. Rather than being a bearish signal, this pattern is a bullish signal, suggesting that the price could start to rise after forming the second inverted shoulder. Traders look for this pattern when they believe the market is about to change from a downtrend to an uptrend. When the price breaks the resistance level that connects the two inverted shoulders, that can be a signal to buy, as the price will likely continue to rise.

Another chart pattern that is quite common is the **triangle**. Triangles form when price moves within an increasingly narrow range, creating a shape that looks like, well, a triangle. There are three main types of triangles: the ascending triangle, the descending triangle, and the symmetrical triangle. The ascending triangle is a bullish pattern that forms when price makes higher lows, but keeps hitting a horizontal resistance level. It is as if price is building up energy before breaking out to the upside. Traders wait for price to break out of resistance to enter a long position.

The descending triangle, on the other hand, is a bearish pattern that forms when the price makes lower highs but keeps touching a horizontal support level. In this case, traders wait for the price to break the support to sell, as it is likely to continue falling. The symmetrical triangle is a neutral pattern, meaning the price could break in either direction, and traders watch closely to see which way it moves before making a decision.

Another pattern that is widely used is the **pennant**. Pennants form when the price moves in a strong trend, either up or down, and then enters a period of consolidation, creating a pattern that looks like a small flag. Traders consider pennants to be continuation patterns, meaning that the price will likely continue in the same direction after consolidation. If the pennant forms in an uptrend, the price is likely to continue rising, and if it forms in a downtrend, the price is likely to continue falling.

In addition to the patterns we have mentioned, there are many other chart patterns that traders use, such as **rectangles**, **wedges**, and **channels**. Rectangles are formed when the price moves in a narrow range, bouncing between a support level and a resistance level. Traders wait for the price to break one of these levels to take a position, as a breakout usually signals a new trend. Wedges are patterns that look similar to triangles, but are steeper and narrower, and can also be bullish or bearish. Channels, on the other hand, are areas where the price moves within two parallel lines, indicating a consistent trend.

The key to taking advantage of chart patterns is patience. Patterns don't form right away, and it can take time before the market gives clear signals. It's important to remember that chart patterns don't guarantee that the price will move in one direction or another; they simply give you an indication of what might happen. As a trader, it's your job to keep an eye out for these patterns and use them as another tool to make informed decisions. Combining chart pattern analysis with other tools, such as volume or technical indicators, can increase your chances of success.

In short, basic chart patterns are figures that form on price charts due to repetitive market behavior. These patterns allow you to identify potential changes in price direction and help you make buy or sell decisions. Whether you're looking for a double top, a head-and-shoulders, or a triangle, the key is to watch the market carefully, be patient, and use these patterns as part of a well-thought-out trading strategy. With time and practice, you'll start to identify these patterns more easily, and they'll become an essential tool in your trading arsenal.

What are Japanese Candles?

Candlesticks are one of the most popular ways to represent price movement on financial charts. They are widely used in trading because they provide a lot of information in a simple, visual way. These candlesticks not only show the price of an asset at a given point in time, but they also reveal how it has changed over a given period of time. Candlesticks allow traders to clearly see whether the price is rising or falling, whether there is buying or selling pressure, and help identify potential entry and exit points in a trade.

Each Japanese candlestick is made up of several key parts: the body and the shadows. The body of the candlestick is the central block, which indicates the range between the opening price and the closing price of an asset in a specific period. If the body is colored green (or white, on some charts), it means that the closing price was higher than the opening price, indicating that the price rose during that period. If the body is red (or black), it means that the closing price was lower than the opening price, indicating that the price fell. This simple color change allows traders to immediately see whether the market is dominated by buyers or sellers.

Shadows, also called wicks or tails, are the lines that extend from the top and bottom of the candle body. These shadows show the highest and lowest prices reached during the period. If a candle has a long shadow pointing up, it means that the price went up quite a bit, but then went down before the close. This can be a sign that buyers tried to push the price up, but didn't have enough strength to keep it there. On the other hand, if the candle has a long shadow pointing down, it means that the price went down a lot during the period, but then went up before the close, which can be a sign that sellers failed to keep the price down.

Each candle represents a time period that can vary depending on the chart you are using. For example, on a one-minute Japanese candlestick chart, each candle shows price movement over a single minute. On an hourly chart, each candle represents one hour of price movement, and so on. This format allows traders to see both short-term price action and broader trends over time. The ability to switch between different time frames is very useful as it provides a more complete view of the market.

One of the most valuable aspects of Japanese candlesticks is that by looking at them, you can identify patterns that can help you predict future market behavior. Some candlestick patterns are bullish signals, meaning they suggest the price could go up, while others are bearish signals, indicating the price could go down. Learning to identify these patterns can make a huge difference in your ability to make informed trading decisions.

A well-known bullish pattern is the so-called **hammer** candlestick. The hammer forms when the price declines sharply for a period, but then recovers and closes near its opening price, creating a long shadow down and a small body at the top. This pattern suggests that sellers dominated at the beginning, but that buyers took control at the end, indicating a possible bullish reversal. Traders see the hammer as a sign that the price might be about to rise, especially if it appears after a downtrend.

On the other hand, one of the most well-known bearish patterns is the so-called shooting star candle. The shooting star is the opposite of the hammer: it has a small body near the bottom and a long shadow up. This shows that buyers tried to push the price higher, but sellers took control and managed to push the price down before the close. Traders see the shooting star as a sign that the price might be about to fall, especially if it appears after an uptrend.

Another candlestick pattern that often appears on charts is the **doji**. A doji is formed when the opening price and the closing price are almost equal, creating a candle with a very small body or no body at all, but with shadows pointing up or down. The doji indicates indecision in the market, as neither buyers nor sellers were able to dominate during the period. Traders interpret the doji as a signal that the market is at a point of equilibrium and that a trend change could be near.

One of the reasons candlesticks are so effective is that they allow you to clearly see the emotions of the market. If you see a lot of candles with large bodies and small shadows, it means that there is a lot of conviction in the direction of the price, either up or down. If the candles have small bodies and long shadows, it indicates that the market is more nervous or indecisive. These visual clues are very useful in understanding market psychology, as they show you whether participants are confident or unsure.

It is important to mention that not all candles or patterns should be taken as definitive signals. Candlesticks are just one part of the bigger picture of technical analysis. It is essential to combine them with other tools, such as support and resistance levels, technical indicators, and volume, to get a clearer idea of what might happen in the market. However, when used correctly, candlesticks are a very powerful tool for traders.

By learning how to read and interpret Japanese candlesticks, you will be equipping yourself with an essential skill for trading. Not only will they help you identify potential entry and exit points, but they will also allow you to see what is happening in the market in real time. With time and practice, you will begin to see patterns and repeating behaviors on the charts that will help you make more informed decisions.

In short, candlesticks are a visual way of depicting price movement that gives traders clear and valuable information. Each candlestick shows the opening price, closing price, highest price, and lowest price in a given period, and its shape and color make it possible to immediately see whether the market is going up or down. By looking at candlestick patterns such as the hammer, shooting star, or doji, traders can identify potential changes in market direction and make more informed decisions. Although candlesticks are only one part of technical analysis, they are an essential tool that can significantly improve your ability to read and understand the market.

How to Use Technical Indicators

Technical indicators are tools that traders use to analyze price movement and predict what might happen in the future. They are a vital part of technical analysis, helping you better understand trends, volatility, and other aspects of the market that aren't always easy to see with the naked eye. Indicators are based on historical price data, such as closing price, opening price, highs and lows, and even trading volume. While indicators don't guarantee that you'll always make the right decision, they do give you an edge by offering signals based on repeating patterns in the market.

One of the most well-known technical indicators is the moving average. The moving average is used to smooth out price fluctuations and help identify the overall direction of the market, also known as the trend. Basically, this indicator takes the average price of an asset over a given period of time. If the price is above the moving average, the market is said to be in an uptrend; if it is below, the market is in a downtrend. Moving averages can be short-term, medium-term, or long-term, depending on how many days they are being averaged over. The longer the time period the moving average covers, the smoother the line will be, but it will also respond more slowly to changes in price.

A variation of the moving average is the exponential moving average. The difference between the simple and exponential moving average is that the latter gives more weight to recent prices, making it more sensitive to short-term changes in the market. Many traders prefer the exponential moving average because it allows them to react faster to potential changes in the trend. For example, if the price crosses above the exponential moving average, it may be a sign that the market is starting an uptrend, and vice versa.

Another widely used technical indicator is the relative strength index, known as RSI. The RSI measures the speed and change of price movements to indicate whether an asset is overbought or oversold. This indicator ranges from 0 to 100, and when the RSI is above 70, it suggests that the asset is overbought, which could indicate a possible drop in price. When the RSI is below 30, it suggests that the asset is oversold, which could signal a buying opportunity. Many traders use the RSI as a signal to enter or exit the market, especially when it is at extreme levels.

The Bollinger Bands indicator is another popular tool that helps traders assess market volatility. Bollinger Bands consist of three lines: a moving average in the center and two additional lines called "bands" that are placed at a certain distance above and below the moving average. These bands expand and contract depending on market volatility. When the price moves close to the upper band, the asset is considered to be overbought, and when it moves close to the lower band, it is said to be oversold. Bollinger Bands are useful for identifying extreme market conditions and can help you predict potential trend reversals.

Volume is another important aspect that traders look at when using technical indicators. Although volume itself is not an indicator, many technical indicators rely on it to confirm buy or sell signals. For example, when the price of an asset is rising and volume is also increasing, it is a sign that the trend could be strong and supported. However, if the price is rising but volume is falling, the trend may not be as strong and the price may soon reverse. Volume-based indicators, such as the volume oscillator or the accumulation/distribution indicator, are useful for seeing if price movements are strongly supported.

The MACD, or Moving Average Convergence/Divergence, is another indicator that many traders use to identify changes in the trend. The MACD is calculated by subtracting a 26-day exponential moving average from a 12-day exponential moving average. Then, a line called the "MACD line" is drawn, and a second line called the "signal line," which is a 9-day exponential moving average of the MACD line. When the MACD line crosses above the signal line, it is a buy signal, and when it crosses below it, it is a sell signal. This indicator is popular because it combines the information from two moving averages and helps traders spot changes in the trend direction.

A key concept to remember when using technical indicators is that none of them are perfect or infallible. Indicators are just tools that give you clues about what might be happening in the market, but they don't tell you for sure what will happen next. For this reason, many traders use multiple indicators at the same time to confirm their analysis. For example, you can use a combination of the moving average, RSI, and Bollinger Bands to get a more complete picture of the situation. If multiple indicators are giving you similar signals, those signals are more likely to be reliable.

It is important not to overload your chart with too many indicators. Sometimes, novice traders fall into the trap of using too many indicators at the same time, which can lead to confusion and conflicting signals. It is best to choose a few indicators that you understand well and that suit your trading style. Also, it is essential to practice using these indicators on a demo account or with small amounts of money before using them on large trades. This will help you become familiar with them and learn how they work in different market conditions.

Another thing to consider is that technical indicators often work best in markets that are trending. When the market moves sideways or without a clear direction, the indicators' signals can become less reliable. In such cases, it is useful to combine technical analysis with fundamental analysis, which focuses on external factors that can affect the price of an asset, such as economic news, earnings reports, or political decisions.

In short, technical indicators are valuable tools that can help you analyze the market and make more informed decisions in your trading. From the moving average and RSI to Bollinger Bands and MACD, each indicator serves its own purpose and gives you a different perspective on price action. By using them in combination and judiciously, you can improve your chances of success in the market. However, remember that no indicator is foolproof, so it is essential to practice and develop your own approach to get the most out of these tools.

Controlling Emotions

Controlling emotions is a fundamental part of trading. Many traders, especially beginners, think that success in this field depends solely on having a good strategy or knowing the markets well. However, the reality is that emotions play a crucial role in the decisions you make, and if you don't learn to manage them, they can lead you to make costly mistakes. From euphoria to fear, frustration and greed, all of these emotions can influence your behavior and cause you to make irrational decisions that go against your long-term interests.

One of the most common emotions traders experience is fear. Fear can appear in different forms: fear of losing money, fear of missing out on a good opportunity, or even fear of making a mistake. This fear can cause you to close a trade early, preventing you from maximizing your profits, or it can cause you to stay out of the market altogether, missing out on opportunities. Learning to control this fear is key to becoming a more efficient trader. Fear is a natural response when it comes to money, but the key is to not let it paralyze you or cause you to make rash decisions. To overcome fear, it is important to have a well-defined plan before entering the market and to trust your analysis.

Another emotion you need to learn to manage is greed. It's easy to get carried away when you see your trades are making profits and think that the market will continue in your favor indefinitely. Greed can cause you to hold a position open longer than necessary, hoping for more profits, which often results in losses when the market changes direction. Greed can also cause you to risk more money than you should on a single trade, believing that a winning streak will continue forever. To prevent greed from controlling you, it's crucial to set clear profit goals and have the discipline to close them when they're reached, without giving in to the temptation of always wanting more.

Frustration is another emotion that affects many traders, especially after a series of losses. It's easy to feel frustrated when things don't go your way, but frustration can lead to impulsive decisions. A common mistake is to try to recoup losses quickly by opening larger or riskier trades. This is known as "revenge trading" in trading, and it often results in more losses. To manage frustration, it's important to accept that losses are a natural part of the process. You can't win on every trade, and that's okay. The important thing is to learn from your mistakes and move on without letting frustration affect your judgment.

Euphoria is another dangerous emotion that can set in after a series of successful trades. When you experience a winning streak, it's natural to feel invincible. However, euphoria can cause you to become careless, failing to follow your trading rules or risking more than you should. Some traders, after having several winning trades, become so confident that they start trading impulsively, without proper analysis or following their trading plan. This overconfidence often leads to significant losses. To prevent euphoria from taking over, it's crucial to stay grounded and remember that the market is unpredictable. Every trade should be treated with the same care, no matter how many wins you've had.

One of the most effective ways to control emotions in trading is to have a well-defined trading plan. This plan should include your profit targets, your risk levels, and the rules you will follow in each trade. By having a clear plan, you reduce the chance of making impulsive decisions based on emotions. If you stick to your plan, it will be easier for you to stay calm and make rational decisions, even when the market is moving. The plan will also help you maintain discipline, which is essential for long-term trading success.

Another useful tool for managing emotions is to set clear limits on each trade. This includes setting a stop-loss, which is the level at which you will close a trade if the market goes against you, and a take-profit, which is the level at which you will close a trade once you have reached your desired profits. By having these predetermined levels, you take the pressure off of having to make decisions in the middle of the trade, which can help reduce the impact of emotions. Additionally, a stop-loss protects you from larger losses, which can reduce fear and anxiety.

Practicing mindfulness can also be a powerful tool for managing emotions in trading. Mindfulness involves being fully present in the moment, without letting your thoughts or emotions take over. By applying mindfulness to trading, you can observe your emotions without letting them control you. If you feel that fear or greed is beginning to influence your decisions, you can take a moment to breathe deeply and reconnect with your trading plan before you act. Practicing mindfulness on a regular basis can also help you become more aware of your emotional patterns and develop a greater ability to stay calm under pressure.

It is important to remember that controlling emotions does not mean ignoring or suppressing them. Emotions are a natural part of being human, and it is impossible to eliminate them completely. The goal is to recognize them when they arise and learn to manage them effectively. This requires practice and self-knowledge. The more you know yourself and how you react in different market situations, the easier it will be to control your emotions in the future.

Finally, it's crucial to keep in mind that trading is a marathon, not a sprint. Successful traders don't get caught up in the emotional ups and downs of each individual trade. Instead, they focus on the bigger picture and strive to be consistent over time. If you can learn to control your emotions, you'll be able to make more rational decisions and be more likely to be successful in the trading world over the long term.

How to Protect Your Capital

Protecting your capital is one of the most important tasks for any trader. No matter how good your strategies are or how much experience you have in the market, if you do not take care of your capital, your days as a trader will be numbered. In this chapter, I will explain in a simple and straightforward way how you can protect your capital and ensure that you can continue trading in the markets in the long term.

First, it is essential to understand that capital is the foundation on which you build your trading career. Without capital, you cannot trade, and without trades, you cannot make profits. Therefore, protecting your capital should always be your number one priority. One of the most effective ways to do this is by using a stop-loss on every trade you make. A stop-loss is an order you give your broker to close a position if the price moves against you to a certain level. This helps you limit your losses and prevent one unfavorable trade from consuming a significant portion of your capital.

The next step in protecting your capital is to understand and properly apply the concept of risk management. Risk management involves determining how much of your capital you are willing to risk on each trade. A general rule of thumb is to not risk more than 1% to 2% of your capital on a single trade. For example, if you have a capital of $10,000, you should not risk more than $100 to $200 per trade. This way, even if you have a series of losses, you will not lose a significant portion of your capital. Risk management is crucial because it allows you to survive the inevitable ups and downs of the market.

Another important strategy to protect your capital is to diversify your investments. Instead of putting all your money into one asset or market, spread your capital across different assets and markets. Diversification reduces risk because not all markets and assets will move in the same direction at the same time. If one of your assets performs poorly, others may perform well, thus offsetting the losses. Diversification is an effective way to minimize risk and protect your capital.

Furthermore, it is essential to avoid over-leveraging. Leverage allows you to control a larger position than your capital would normally allow. While this can magnify your profits, it can also amplify your losses. If you use too much leverage and the market moves against you, you could lose a significant portion of your capital very quickly. Therefore, it is important to use leverage with caution and make sure you understand the associated risks before using it in your trading.

Another crucial technique to protect your capital is to keep a trading journal. In this journal, you should record all your trades, including entry and exit details, the reasons behind each trade, and the results obtained. By reviewing your trading journal regularly, you will be able to identify patterns in your behavior and trading decisions. This will allow you to learn from your mistakes and adjust your strategies to improve your results. A trading journal provides you with an objective view of your performance and helps you make more informed decisions in the future.

Furthermore, it is important to maintain a disciplined mindset and avoid being carried away by emotions. Fear and greed are two emotions that can lead you to make irrational decisions that put your capital at risk. To maintain discipline, always follow your trading plan and do not deviate from your established rules, no matter how you feel at the moment. Staying calm and objective will allow you to make more rational decisions and protect your capital from emotional influences.

Continuing education is another key aspect of protecting your capital. The world of trading is constantly evolving, and what works today may not work tomorrow. Always stay informed and up-to-date on the latest trading trends, tools, and strategies. Attend seminars, read books, and follow experienced traders to learn from their experiences. The more informed you are, the better equipped you will be to make decisions that protect your capital.

It's also important to have a contingency plan. Sometimes, despite all your precautions, things can go wrong. Having a contingency plan means you're prepared for any eventuality and know how to react if the market moves against you unexpectedly. This can include having extra funds set aside for emergencies or knowing when it's time to step away and reevaluate your strategy.

Finally, remember that trading is a long-term career. Don't worry about making a lot of money quickly. Instead, focus on protecting your capital and building a solid foundation for your trading. If you can avoid big losses and keep your capital intact, you'll have many more opportunities to make profits in the future. Patience and prudence are your best allies in trading.

In short, protecting your capital involves using stop-losses, proper risk management, diversification, avoiding over-leverage, keeping a trading journal, controlling emotions, continuing to educate yourself, having a contingency plan, and adopting a long-term mindset. By following these principles, you will be in a better position to protect your capital and succeed in the trading world in the long term. Always remember that your capital is the foundation of your trading career, and protecting it should be your number one priority.

The Power of Trends

The power of trends is a fundamental concept in the world of trading. Trends are the direction in which the market moves over a period of time. They can be up, down, or sideways. Understanding trends and how to take advantage of them can make a huge difference in your success as a trader. In this chapter, we will explore what trends are, why they are important, and how you can use them to your advantage in simple and effective ways.

An uptrend occurs when prices are steadily rising. This means that buyers are dominating the market and pushing prices up. On the other hand, a downtrend occurs when prices are steadily falling, indicating that sellers are in control and are driving prices down. Finally, a sideways trend occurs when prices move in a narrow range, with no clear direction up or down. During these periods, neither buyers nor sellers have clear control of the market.

Why are trends important? Because trading with a trend puts you in an advantageous position. When you follow the direction of the market, you are aligned with the prevailing force, which increases your chances of success. For example, if you are in an uptrend, opening a buy position will allow you to profit from the general upward movement. Similarly, in a downtrend, opening a sell position will help you take advantage of the general downward direction. Going against the trend, on the other hand, can be risky and often results in losses.

Identifying a trend can seem complicated at first, but there are some tools and techniques that can help you. One of the simplest ways is to look at price charts and look for patterns of higher highs and lower lows. In an uptrend, you'll see a series of higher highs and higher lows. In a downtrend, you'll see a series of lower highs and lower lows. In a sideways trend, the highs and lows will be more or less at the same level.

In addition to looking at charts, you can use tools like moving averages to identify trends. A moving average is a line on a chart that shows the average price of an asset over a specific period of time. When the price is above the moving average, it generally indicates an upward trend. When the price is below the moving average, it suggests a downward trend. Moving averages can help you smooth out market fluctuations and more clearly see the general direction of price movement.

Another useful tool for identifying trends is the use of trend lines. A trend line is a straight line drawn on a price chart to connect a series of highs or lows. In an uptrend, you draw a trend line connecting the lower lows. In a downtrend, you draw a trend line connecting the higher highs. These lines can serve as a visual guide to help you see and follow the direction of the market.

Once you've identified a trend, it's important to know how to trade with it. In an uptrend, you'll look for opportunities to buy. This may involve entering the market after a pullback, when the price temporarily drops before resuming its upward move. In a downtrend, you'll look for opportunities to sell. This may mean entering the market after a rally, when the price temporarily rises before continuing its downward move. Trading with the trend helps you take advantage of larger market moves and minimize the risk of losses.

It is also crucial to understand that trends do not last forever. Eventually, every trend runs out of steam and the market changes direction. That is why, in addition to identifying and following trends, you also need to keep an eye out for trend reversal signals. These signals can include reversal patterns on charts, such as double tops or double bottoms, and changes in technical indicators, such as moving average crossovers. Keeping an eye out for these signals will allow you to adjust your trades and protect your profits.

In addition to technical tools, it is important to consider fundamental factors that can influence trends. Economic news, political events, and changes in monetary policy are just a few examples of factors that can affect market direction. Staying informed about these events and understanding how they can impact prices will give you an added advantage in identifying and following trends.

Trading with trends not only helps you take advantage of market movements, but it can also simplify your decision-making process. When you trade with the trend, you reduce the need to predict every little movement in the market. Instead, you can focus on following the general direction and adjusting your trades accordingly. This can reduce stress and uncertainty, making trading a more manageable and enjoyable experience.

Also, it is important to keep in mind that trends can be of different magnitudes and durations. Some trends may last only a few days or weeks, while others may persist for months or even years. Depending on your trading style and goals, you can focus on short-term, medium-term, or long-term trends. The important thing is to adapt your strategy to the trend you are following and be flexible to adjust it when the market changes.

Finally, patience and discipline are essential when trading trends. It won't always be easy to identify and follow a trend, and there will be times when the market is unpredictable.

However, if you maintain a consistent focus and follow your trading rules, you will increase your chances of success. Remember that trading is a marathon, not a sprint, and patience and discipline are key to achieving your long-term goals.

In short, the power of trends lies in their ability to guide your trading decisions and increase your chances of success. Identifying and following trends puts you in alignment with the prevailing force of the market, which can help you maximize your profits and minimize your losses. Using tools such as price charts, moving averages, and trend lines, you can effectively identify and follow trends. Furthermore, by considering fundamental factors and staying informed, you can adjust your trading as needed. With patience and discipline, you can harness the power of trends and improve your trading performance.

Common Beginner Mistakes

The trading path is full of challenges, especially for beginners. Making mistakes is part of the learning process, but there are some common mistakes that new traders tend to make over and over again. In this chapter, we're going to explore these mistakes and how you can avoid them. Understanding these mistakes and learning from them will help you become a more successful and consistent trader. Below, I'll explain in a simple and straightforward way the most common mistakes beginners make.

One of the most common mistakes is not having a trading plan. A trading plan is essential because it gives you a clear guide of what you should do in different market situations. Without a plan, it is easy to make impulsive decisions based on emotions such as fear or greed. A good trading plan should include your financial goals, the strategies you are going to use, and the rules for managing risk. Taking the time to develop and follow a trading plan can make a huge difference in your success.

Another common mistake is not using a stop-loss. A stop-loss is an order that closes your trade automatically if the price moves against you to a certain level. Many beginners do not use a stop-loss because they believe that the price will return in their favor. However, not using a stop-loss can lead to significant and rapid losses. You should always use a stop-loss on every trade to limit your losses and protect your capital.

Over-leveraging is another common mistake. Leverage allows you to control a larger position than your capital would normally allow. While this can magnify your profits, it can also amplify your losses. Many beginners use too much leverage because they want to make a lot of money quickly. However, this is very risky and can lead to significant losses. It is important to use leverage with caution and make sure you understand the risks before using it.

Lack of education and preparation is also a serious mistake. Many beginners jump into trading without having learned enough about how the market works. It is crucial to take the time to educate yourself and understand the basics of trading before you begin. This includes learning about technical and fundamental analysis, risk management, and the different trading strategies. The more informed you are, the better decisions you can make.

Another common mistake is to get carried away by emotions. Fear and greed are two emotions that can lead you to make irrational decisions. For example, fear can make you close a trade prematurely, while greed can make you hold a position open for too long, hoping for more profit. It is important to stay calm and disciplined, and always follow your trading plan, no matter how you feel at the moment.

Many beginners also tend to overtrade. Overtrading means making too many trades in a short period of time. This can happen because the trader is eager to make money or because he or she believes that he or she should always be active in the market. However, overtrading can lead to mistakes and unnecessary losses. It is better to be selective with your trades and wait for the best opportunities.

Failing to keep a record of your trades is another common mistake. A trading journal is a valuable tool that allows you to record all the details of your trades, including the reasons behind each trade and the results obtained. By reviewing your trading journal, you will be able to identify patterns in your trading behavior and decisions, allowing you to learn from your mistakes and improve your strategies.

Lack of patience is another common problem. Many beginners want to see immediate results and get frustrated when they don't make profits quickly. Trading is a long-term career, and it is important to be patient and not expect instant results. Patience will allow you to wait for the best opportunities and avoid making impulsive decisions.

Furthermore, many beginners do not diversify their investments. Putting all your money into one asset or market is very risky, because if that asset or market performs poorly, you could lose a significant portion of your capital. Diversifying your investments, by spreading your capital across different assets and markets, will help you minimize risk and protect your capital.

Finally, a common mistake is not adapting to changing market conditions. The market is constantly evolving, and what works today may not work tomorrow. It is important to be flexible and willing to adjust your strategies as needed. Always stay informed about the latest trends and develop the ability to adapt to changing market conditions.

In summary, the most common mistakes beginners make include not having a trading plan, not using a stop-loss, using too much leverage, lack of education and preparation, being carried away by emotions, overtrading, not keeping a trading record, lack of patience, not diversifying investments, and not adapting to changing market conditions. By understanding these mistakes and learning from them, you will be able to improve your performance as a trader and increase your chances of long-term success. Remember that trading is a continuous learning process, and every mistake is an opportunity to grow and improve.

How to Create Your First Trading Plan

Creating your first trading plan is an essential step in becoming a successful trader. A trading plan is like a map that guides you through the market, helping you make informed decisions and maintain discipline. Without a plan, it's easy to get carried away by emotions and make costly mistakes. In this chapter, I'll explain in a simple and straightforward way how to create your first trading plan. Throughout this process, you'll learn how to set clear goals, define your strategies, and manage your risk effectively.

The first step in creating your trading plan is to set your goals. It's important to be clear about what you hope to achieve from trading. Your goals can be short-, medium-, and long-term. For example, you might aim to make a certain amount of money each month, learn a new trading strategy, or simply not lose money while you learn. It's critical that your goals are realistic and achievable. Setting goals that are too ambitious can lead to frustration and risky decisions.

Once you have your goals clear, it's time to define your trading style. There are different trading styles, and each has its own characteristics and requirements. Some of the most common styles include day trading, swing trading, and long-term trading. Day trading involves opening and closing trades within the same day, which requires constant attention and quick decision making. Swing trading involves holding trades for several days or weeks, which allows you to take advantage of larger market movements. Long-term trading involves holding trades for months or even years, which requires patience and a long-term view. Define which style best suits your personality, time availability, and goals.

After you have defined your trading style, you need to decide which markets you are going to trade in. There are many financial markets you can participate in, such as the stock market, the forex market, the futures market, and the cryptocurrency market. Each market has its own characteristics, advantages, and disadvantages. For example, the stock market is known for its stability and the possibility of earning dividends, while the forex market is known for its high liquidity and the possibility of trading 24 hours a day. Research the different markets and choose the one that best suits your goals and trading style.

Once you have decided which markets you will trade, it is time to define your trading strategies. A trading strategy is a set of rules and criteria that you use to make buying and selling decisions. Your strategy should include both technical and fundamental criteria. Technical criteria are based on the analysis of charts and price patterns, while fundamental criteria are based on the analysis of news and economic events. For example, you might have a strategy that tells you to buy when the price crosses above a moving average and sell when the price crosses below another moving average. Define your strategies clearly and be sure to test them on a demo account before using them with real money.

Risk management is another crucial component of your trading plan. Risk management involves defining how much you are willing to lose on each trade and how you are going to protect your capital. A common rule of thumb is to not risk more than one or two percent of your capital on a single trade. This will help you limit your losses and protect your capital in the long run. You should also define how you are going to use stop-loss and take-profit orders. A stop-loss order closes your trade automatically if the price moves against you to a certain level, limiting your losses. A take-profit order closes your trade automatically when the price reaches a target level, locking in your profits.

In addition to risk management, it is important to define how you are going to manage your capital. Capital management involves deciding how much money you are going to allocate to trading and how you are going to allocate it between different trades. It is advisable not to invest all your capital in a single trade, but to diversify it across several trades to reduce risk. You should also define how you are going to reinvest your profits and how you are going to handle losses. Capital management is essential to maintaining the stability and sustainability of your trading in the long term.

An important part of your trading plan is to keep a detailed record of all your trades. A trading journal allows you to record the details of each trade, including the reasons behind each decision, the results achieved, and the lessons learned. By reviewing your trading journal regularly, you will be able to identify patterns in your trading behavior and decisions, allowing you to learn from your mistakes and improve your strategies. A trading journal is a valuable tool for continued growth and development as a trader.

Finally, it is crucial to maintain discipline and patience when following your trading plan. The market can be volatile and unpredictable, and there will be times when your trades do not go as you expected. It is important to remain calm and not get carried away by emotions. Always follow your trading plan, adjust your strategies as needed, and learn from each experience. Patience and discipline are key to long-term success in trading.

In summary, creating your first trading plan involves setting clear goals, defining your trading style, choosing the markets you will trade, developing your trading strategies, managing risk and capital, keeping detailed records of your trades, and maintaining discipline and patience. Taking the time to develop and follow a trading plan will help you make informed decisions, maintain discipline, and increase your chances of trading success. Remember that trading is a continuous learning process, and each step you take to improve your trading plan will bring you closer to your goals.

The Importance of Discipline in Trading

Discipline is one of the most important pillars of trading success. Without discipline, even the best strategies and most detailed plans can fail. But what is discipline in the context of trading and why is it so crucial? In this chapter, we are going to explore the importance of discipline in trading, how to cultivate and maintain it, and how it can make a significant difference to your results. We will use simple words to keep everything clear and straightforward, and we will make the topic a bit entertaining so that you can enjoy learning.

At its core, trading discipline refers to the ability to stick to your trading plan no matter the circumstances. This means sticking to the rules and strategies you've set out, even when the market gets volatile or when emotions start to get in the way. Discipline is what stops you from making impulsive decisions based on fear or greed, and keeps you focused on your long-term goals.

One of the first reasons why discipline is so important is that it helps minimize losses. When you trade without discipline, it's easy to panic and close a trade prematurely, or hold onto a losing position in the hope that the market will recover. Both of these actions can lead to significant losses. By maintaining discipline, you ensure that you follow your risk management rules, which helps you limit losses and protect your capital.

Discipline is also crucial to consistently taking advantage of opportunities. The market presents many opportunities, but not all of them are good. Discipline allows you to wait for the best opportunities and act only when conditions meet your predefined criteria. Not only does this increase your chances of success, but it also helps you avoid overtrading, which is trading too much and unnecessarily.

Additionally, discipline helps you stay calm during times of high volatility. The market can be unpredictable and emotionally challenging. Without discipline, it's easy to be driven by fear when prices fall or greed when prices rise rapidly. Maintaining discipline allows you to make decisions based on your analysis and trading plan, rather than reacting impulsively to market movements.

Cultivating trading discipline begins with creating a detailed trading plan. This plan should include your goals, strategies, risk management rules, and a system for keeping track of your trades. Once you have this plan, it's crucial to follow it rigorously. It can be helpful to think of your trading plan as a contract with yourself, committing to sticking to it no matter what happens.

Another important aspect of discipline is patience. Trading is not a get-rich-quick race. It requires time, effort, and the ability to wait for the right opportunities. Patience allows you to stay focused and avoid making rash decisions. Remember that it is better to not trade than to make a trade that does not meet your criteria.

Maintaining discipline also involves learning to manage your emotions. Trading can be stressful, and it's normal to feel fear or greed. However, it's important not to let these emotions dictate your decisions. Techniques such as meditation, regular exercise, and taking breaks can help you stay calm and mentally clear. Additionally, keeping a trading journal where you record your emotions and reflect on your decisions can be very helpful in improving your self-control.

Consistency is another key reason for the importance of discipline. By following your trading plan consistently, you can objectively evaluate your results and adjust your strategies as needed. If you constantly change your approaches and rules, it will be difficult to identify what is working and what is not. Consistency allows you to accumulate data and experiences that are essential to improving your trading skills.

Finally, trading discipline fosters confidence. When you stick to your plan and see positive results, even if they are small, you begin to trust your skills and approach more. This confidence is essential to maintaining motivation and perseverance over time. Confidence in yourself and your plan allows you to face market challenges with a positive and determined attitude.

In conclusion, discipline is essential for trading success. It helps you minimize losses, take advantage of opportunities, stay calm in times of volatility, and build confidence and consistency in your trading. Cultivating and maintaining discipline requires conscious and continuous effort, but the long-term benefits make it worth it. Always remember that trading is a marathon, not a sprint. Discipline is your best ally on this journey to financial success.

Basic Strategies for Beginners

Basic trading strategies for beginners are essential to build a solid foundation and start your trading journey effectively and safely. In this chapter, we are going to explore some of the simplest and most effective strategies that beginners can use. These strategies will help you understand how the market works, make informed decisions, and manage your risk appropriately. We will use simple words to explain each strategy in a straightforward and extensive manner, making sure that the content is a bit entertaining to keep you interested.

One of the most common and easiest to understand strategies is the trend strategy. This strategy is based on the idea that asset prices tend to move in a general direction over a period of time. There are three types of trends: uptrend, downtrend, and sideways. An uptrend is when prices are going up, a downtrend is when prices are going down, and a sideways trend is when prices are moving in a range with no clear direction. The key to this strategy is identifying the direction of the trend and trading in that direction. For example, if the market is in an uptrend, you will look for opportunities to buy. If it is in a downtrend, you will look for opportunities to sell. Tools like moving averages can help you identify these trends more clearly.

Another basic strategy is breakout trading. This strategy focuses on identifying key support and resistance levels on price charts. Support is a level where prices tend to stop and bounce upward, while resistance is a level where prices tend to stop and bounce downward. When price breaks above a resistance or below a support, it can signal the beginning of a strong move in the direction of the breakout. For example, if price breaks above a resistance, you might consider buying, expecting the price to continue rising. Conversely, if price breaks below a support, you might consider selling, expecting the price to continue falling. It is important to confirm the breakout with volume or other technical indicators to increase the probability of success.

The pullback strategy is another popular technique among beginners. This strategy is based on the idea that prices never move in a straight line, but rather experience pullbacks or corrections before continuing in the direction of the main trend. Pullbacks are opportunities to enter a trade at a better price. For example, if the market is in an uptrend, you can wait for a pullback towards a support level before buying. Similarly, in a downtrend, you can wait for a pullback towards a resistance level before selling. Fibonacci retracement levels are common tools used to identify these potential entry points.

Scalping is another strategy that many beginners find interesting. Scalping involves making many small trades throughout the day to capture small profits. This strategy requires constant attention and quick decision making as trades usually last only a few minutes. The goal is to take advantage of small price movements. While it can be a profitable strategy, it is also risky and can be tiring. It is crucial to have a solid risk management plan and be disciplined to avoid big losses.

Another basic strategy that beginners can use is swing trading. Swing trading focuses on capturing price movements that occur over several days or weeks. Unlike day trading, where trades are opened and closed on the same day, swing trading allows more time for trades to develop. This strategy is ideal for those who cannot be in front of a screen all day. Swing traders look for chart patterns and use technical indicators to identify entry and exit points. Patience is key in swing trading, as it is all about waiting for the right time to enter and exit a trade.

News trading is another strategy that can be used by beginners. This strategy is based on the idea that important events and news can have a significant impact on asset prices. News traders keep an eye on economic reports, earnings announcements, changes in central bank policies, and other relevant events. The key to this strategy is to act quickly and take advantage of the momentum that news generates. However, it is important to note that news trading can be volatile and risky, so good risk management is essential.

Finally, a simple yet effective strategy is the use of moving averages. Moving averages are indicators that show the average price of an asset over a specific period of time. There are different types of moving averages, such as the simple moving average and the exponential moving average. These tools can help smooth out price fluctuations and identify trend direction. For example, a common strategy is to use a 50-day moving average and a 200-day moving average. When the 50-day moving average crosses above the 200-day moving average, it is a buy signal, and when it crosses below it, it is a sell signal. This strategy is easy to understand and can be a good way to get started in trading.

In conclusion, there are many basic strategies that beginners can use to get started in trading. From identifying trends and breakouts to using retracements and moving averages, each strategy has its own advantages and disadvantages. It is important to try out different approaches, keep a record of your trades, and adjust your strategies as needed. Always remember that the key to trading success is discipline, risk management, and patience. With time and practice, you will be able to develop your own trading style and improve your skills.

The Power of Demo Accounts

Demo accounts are a powerful tool for anyone just starting out in the world of trading. These accounts allow beginners to practice and get familiar with the financial markets without risking real money. In this chapter, we're going to explore what demo accounts are, how they work, and why they're so valuable to novice traders. We'll use simple words and straightforward explanations to make sure everything is clear and entertaining.

A demo account is basically a simulation of a real trading account. Trading platforms offer demo accounts so that users can practice trading in a safe environment. In a demo account, you are provided with a fictitious amount of money that you can use to trade on the financial markets. Although the money is fictitious, the prices and market movements are real, making the experience very similar to trading with a real account.

The main benefit of a demo account is that it allows you to learn without risk. When you are just starting out in trading, it is easy to make mistakes. By using a demo account, you can experiment and test different strategies without the pressure of losing real money. This gives you the freedom to make mistakes and learn from them without suffering financial consequences. It is like a training camp where you can develop your skills before entering the real battlefield.

Demo accounts are also a great way to familiarize yourself with the trading platform. Each trading platform has its own features and tools. Using a demo account allows you to explore all of these features and learn how to use them effectively. You can practice opening and closing trades, setting alerts, using technical indicators, and much more. The more familiar you are with the platform, the more comfortable you will feel when you start trading with real money.

Another important aspect of demo accounts is that they allow you to test and refine your trading strategies. In trading, having a clear strategy is crucial to success. Without a strategy, it's easy to make impulsive decisions based on emotions rather than rational analysis.

With a demo account, you can test out different strategies and see which ones work best for you. You can tweak and refine your methods until you feel confident that you have an effective approach.

In addition, demo accounts allow you to practice risk management. Risk management is a vital part of trading. It is about how you protect your capital and minimize losses when the market does not move in your favor. On a demo account, you can practice how to set stop-loss and take-profit, how to determine the appropriate position size, and how to diversify your investments. All of this will help you develop a disciplined mindset and learn to control your emotions, which is essential for long-term success.

Demo accounts are also useful for evaluating your progress. When you start trading on a demo account, you can keep track of your trades and analyze your results. This allows you to identify patterns in your decisions and see where you can improve. You can review your mistakes and learn from them, which will help you avoid making the same mistakes in the future. Evaluating your progress on a constant basis will allow you to continuously improve your trading skills.

It is important to mention that although demo accounts are an invaluable tool for beginners, there are some differences between trading on a demo account and a real account. The main difference is trading psychology. When you trade on a demo account, you do not have the stress of risking your own money. This can lead to more relaxed and less impulsive decisions. However, when you trade on a real account, the fear of losing money and greed can influence your decisions. That is why it is important to not only practice on a demo account, but also be prepared to manage your emotions when you move to a real account.

In conclusion, demo accounts are an essential tool for anyone who wants to learn how to trade. They allow you to practice risk-free, familiarize yourself with the trading platform, test and refine your strategies, practice risk management, and evaluate your progress. While there are differences between trading on a demo account and a real account, the time you spend practicing on a demo account will better prepare you to face the challenges of trading with real money. Make the most of this tool and use the time on the demo account to develop your skills and build a solid foundation for your future trading career.

The Path to Real Trading

The road to real trading is an exciting and challenging journey. For many beginners, the transition from a demo account to a live account can seem like a big leap. However, with proper preparation and the right mindset, this step can be made more manageable and less stressful. In this chapter, we will explore the key steps you need to take to prepare for real trading, from consolidating your knowledge to managing your emotions. We will use simple words and straightforward explanations to keep everything clear and entertaining.

The first step on the road to real trading is to consolidate your knowledge. Before risking your money, it is essential that you have a good understanding of the basics of trading. This includes knowing how financial markets work, understanding the importance of technical and fundamental analysis, and familiarizing yourself with trading tools and strategies. If you still feel unsure about any of these aspects, it is important to take the time to learn and practice more on your demo account. Continuing education is key in trading, and you should never stop learning.

Once you feel comfortable with your knowledge, the next step is to develop a solid trading plan. A trading plan is like a map that guides your decisions in the market. It should include your financial goals, your risk tolerance, your entry and exit strategies, and your money management rules. Having a plan helps you maintain discipline and make decisions based on analysis rather than emotion. It is important that your trading plan is clear and detailed, and that you follow it consistently.

Risk management is another crucial aspect on the path to real trading. When you trade with real money, the risk of losing is always a possibility. To protect your capital, you need to learn how to manage risk effectively. This includes setting loss limits, also known as stop-losses, for each trade, and never risking more than you can afford to lose. Additionally, it is advisable to diversify your investments to reduce risk. Don't put all your eggs in one basket; spread your capital across different assets to minimize potential losses.

The next step is to open a real account with a reliable broker. Choosing a broker is an important decision as it will affect your trading experience. Make sure you choose a broker that is regulated and offers favorable trading conditions, such as low transaction costs, an easy-to-use trading platform, and good customer service. Do your research before making a decision and, if possible, check out reviews from other traders. Once you have chosen a broker, open a real account and deposit an amount of money that you are willing to risk.

Before you start trading on your live account, it is important to make a gradual transition from the demo account. Don't just jump into live trading with large amounts of money. Start with small trades and increase your position size gradually as you gain confidence and experience. This will help you adapt to the psychological pressure of trading with real money and minimize the impact of initial mistakes.

Trading psychology is an aspect that cannot be underestimated. Trading with real money can be emotionally challenging. Fear and greed are common emotions that can affect your decisions. To manage these emotions, it is essential to maintain a disciplined mindset and follow your trading plan to the letter. Avoid making impulsive decisions and learn to accept losses as part of the process. Remember that trading is a marathon, not a sprint, and patience is a virtue that will help you succeed in the long run.

Additionally, it is important to keep a record of all your trades. Keep a trading journal where you write down every trade you make, including the reasons for the trade, the results, and the lessons learned. This record will allow you to analyze your mistakes and successes, and help you continually improve your trading skills. Reviewing your trading journal regularly is a great way to identify patterns in your behavior and adjust your strategy accordingly.

Another aspect to consider is constantly updating your knowledge. Financial markets are constantly changing, and what works today may not work tomorrow. Keep up with economic news, continue learning about new trading strategies and techniques, and participate in trading communities to exchange ideas and experiences. Continuing education is an essential part of trading success.

Finally, it's important to have a long-term mindset. Real trading is not a get-rich-quick scheme. It's a process that requires time, effort, and dedication. Don't be discouraged by initial losses and keep a realistic outlook on your expectations. With time and practice, you can improve your skills and increase your chances of success.

In conclusion, the path to real trading is a process that requires preparation, discipline, and the right mindset. Consolidate your knowledge, develop a solid trading plan, manage risk effectively, make a gradual transition from the demo account, keep a record of your trades, constantly update your knowledge, and have a long-term mindset. With these steps, you will be better prepared to face the challenges of real trading and increase your chances of success in the market.

www.ingramcontent.com/pod-product-compliance
Lightning Source LLC
Chambersburg PA
CBHW022146150726

47992CB00002B/787